"Smile," Says Little Crocodile

by Jane Belk Moncure
illustrated by Linda Hohag
and Lori Jacobson

Published by

THE CHILD'S WORLD

Mankato, Minnesota

The Library —
A Magic Castle

Come to the magic castle
When you are growing tall.
Rows upon rows of Word Windows
Line every single wall.
They reach up high,
As high as the sky,
And you want to open them all.
For every time you open one,
A new adventure has begun.

Maria opened
a Word Window.
Here is what she read.

"I like to smile," says Crocodile.

"When I smile, guess what I see?
A smile comes smiling back at me."

"The doctor helps me keep my smile,"
says the little crocodile.

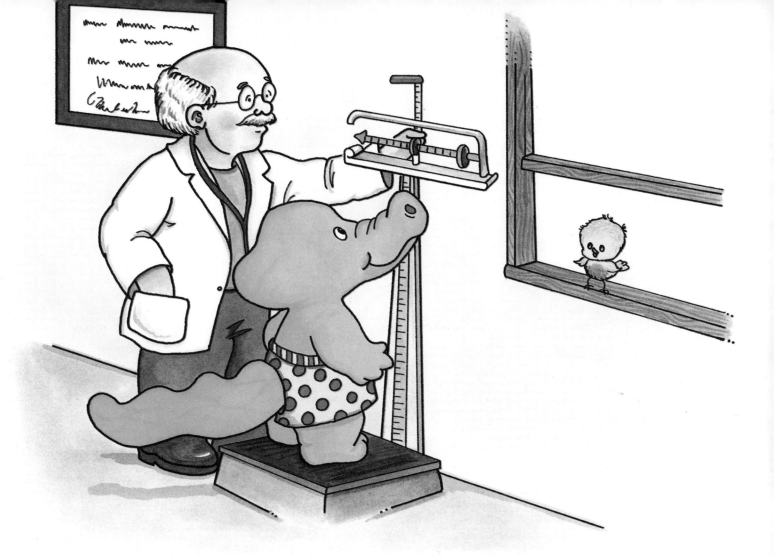

"He keeps me well from head to toe.
My smile gets bigger as I grow."

"Good food helps me keep my smile,"
says the little crocodile.

"I eat apples and celery for snacks and treats, instead of so many gooey sweets."

"Exercise helps me keep my smile,"
says the little crocodile. "I jog . . .

I climb, I jump rope, too."

"I like to hike . . .

and ride my bike. Exercise keeps
me smiling all day through."

"Another way I keep a smile is by dressing
for the weather," says Crocodile.

"I wear boots and a snowsuit in the snow
so I stay warm from head to toe."

"Sniffles and sneezes take smiles away,
so I try to stay dry on a rainy day."

"Another way I keep my smile is by visiting the dentist," says Crocodile.

"I open my mouth very wide to let the dentist peek inside.

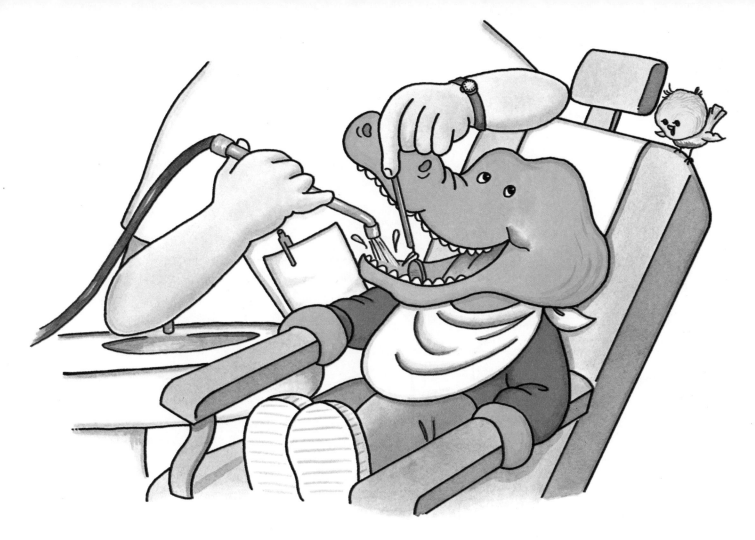

"He cleans my teeth so they look like new.
And my crocodile smile comes shining
through."

"A toothbrush is a smile's good friend.
I brush my teeth from end to end.

"I brush my teeth row-by-row,
just the way they grow.

"I brush up from the bottom . . .

down from the top . . .

and 'round in circles, before I stop."

"I take care of my health the whole year through.

"That is why my crocodile smile is the happiest, snappiest smile of all.
You can have one, too!"

Here's how you can have a happy, snappy crocodile smile.

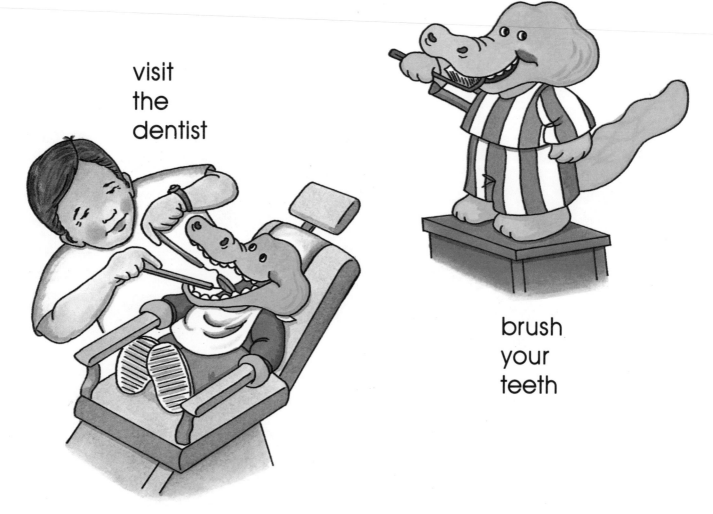

visit
the
dentist

brush
your
teeth

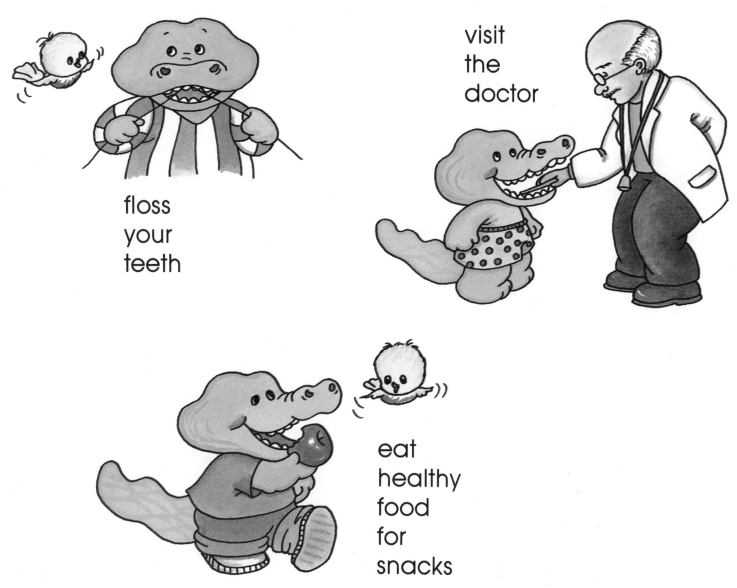

floss
your
teeth

visit
the
doctor

eat
healthy
food
for
snacks

dress for
the
weather

exercise
every day